Design: Judith Chant and Alison Lee
Recipe Photography: Peter Barry
Jacket and Illustration Artwork: Jane Winton, courtesy of
Bernard Thornton Artists, London
Editors: Jillian Stewart and Kate Cranshaw

CLB 4261
Published by Grange Books, an imprint of Grange Books PLC,
The Grange, Grange Yard, London, SE1 3AG
© 1995 CLB Publishing, Godalming, Surrey, England.
All rights reserved
Printed and bound in Singapore
Published 1995
ISBN 1-85627-573-6

THE
LITTLE BOOK
· OF ·

Cooking For Two

*An invaluable collection of
delicious recipes for creative and
informal dining.*

Grange BOOKS

Introduction

Choosing just what to cook when there are only two of you to cook for can be difficult. Something requiring a great deal of care and attention often does not seem worthwhile, or quite likely you just do not have the time. For many people, a lack of time means turning to supermarket convenience meals rather than actually preparing something themselves. This situation, though understandable, is far from ideal. The majority of convenience meals are expensive, not always healthy, and leave a lot to be desired in terms of taste.

The secret to preparing meals for two is to incorporate an unusual flavour or ingredient, something a little out of the ordinary in the form of, for example, herbs, spices, and dried fruit and nuts, all of which can be conveniently kept in the store cupboard ready for use.

When cooking for two, the best dishes to choose for everyday meals, particularly if you are starting after a day's work, are those that are quick and easy to prepare – the more lengthy ones can always be saved for the weekend. Rice, pasta and salads make good accompaniments for convenient mid-week meals. If meat is on the menu, the most appropriate cuts are quick-cooking ones such as steaks, chops and escalopes. Chicken is particularly good as it is quick and easy to cook and is available in so many different cuts. Fish is also an ideal buy, as it is available ready-prepared and is both healthy and quick to cook.

There are some aspects of our high-tech modern world that actually make it far easier to shop and cook for two than ever before. Self-service shopping and weighing machines in the shops enable the shopper to buy exactly the amount they require, such as a few items of fruit, or a single head of broccoli, or whatever, without incurring the shopkeeper's wrath. Also, once home with the shopping, the microwave can be of tremendous help, particularly when cooking vegetables and reheating precooked meals. Of course, the freezer, too, has obvious advantages when dealing with small quantities. Large quantities of delicious dishes can be made, divided into portions and frozen for later use. This allows you to maximise your time with the minimum of effort.

The cook dealing with small amounts generally does not want to spend too long preparing complex meals, but he or she is likely to want to make something enjoyable to linger over, especially if cooking for a partner, and that is what this book is all about. Armed with this collection of rather special recipes, cooking for two will become a real pleasure.

Fried Squid

SERVES 2
Serve this sweet and delicious seafood as a starter.
It's easier to prepare than you think!

PREPARATION: 20 mins
COOKING: 3 mins per batch

340g/12oz small, fresh squid
30g/1oz plain flour
Salt and pepper
Oil for deep-frying
Lemon wedges and parsley for garnishing

---

1. Hold the body of the squid with one hand and the head with the other and pull gently to separate. Remove the intestines and the quill, which is clear and plastic-like. Rinse the body of the squid inside and outside under cold running water.

2. Cut the tentacles from the head, just above

Step 2 Cut the tentacles from the head just above the eye and separate them into individual pieces.

Step 3 Remove the outer skin from the body of the squid and cut the body into thin rings.

the eye. Separate into individual tentacles.

3. Remove the brownish or purplish outer skin from the body of the squid and cut the flesh into 5mm/¼-inch rings.

4. Mix the flour, salt and pepper together on a sheet of paper or in a shallow dish. Toss the rings of squid and the tentacles in the flour mixture to coat. Heat the oil to 180°C/350°F and fry the squid, about 6 pieces at a time, saving the tentacles until last. Cook for about 3 minutes or until lightly browned and crisp. Remove them from the oil with a slotted spoon and drain on kitchen paper. Sprinkle lightly with salt and continue with the remaining squid. Place on serving dishes and garnish each with lemon and parsley.

Imperial Asparagus

SERVES 2

This makes a lovely summer dish and is ideal for a special occasion as a starter or side dish.

PREPARATION: 15 mins
COOKING: 20 mins

460g/1lb asparagus
25g/¾oz butter or margarine
1½ tbsps flour
140ml/¼ pint chicken stock
75ml/2½ fl oz white wine
1 egg yolk
2 tbsps double cream
Salt and white pepper
Pinch sugar, optional

---

1. Break off the woody ends of the asparagus then trim the spears to make them all the same length. Using a swivel vegetable peeler, pare the stalks up to the tips.

2. Tie the spears in a loose bundle and stand them upright in a deep saucepan of lightly salted boiling water. Alternatively, place the spears in a large frying pan of boiling salted water and place half on and half off the heat, with the tips of the asparagus off the heat.

3. Cook, uncovered, for about 12-15 minutes, or until the asparagus is tender. Drain and keep the asparagus warm in a covered serving dish.

4. Melt the butter in a heavy-based saucepan and stir in the flour off the heat. Gradually beat in the stock and add the wine. Stir until the sauce is smooth and then place over a low heat.

5. Bring the sauce to the boil, stirring constantly, and allow to boil for about 1-2 minutes, or until thickened.

6. Beat the egg yolk and cream together and add a few spoonfuls of the hot sauce. Return the egg and cream mixture to the pan, stirring constantly. Reheat if necessary, but do not allow the sauce to boil. Add salt and white pepper and a pinch of sugar if wished. Pour over the asparagus and serve immediately.

Step 1 Hold the trimmed asparagus in your hand and take off the skin in thin strips using a swivel vegetable peeler.

Creamy Dressed Crab

SERVES 2

This makes a delicious warm weather salad for lunches, or light suppers.

PREPARATION: 45 mins
COOKING: 10 mins

---

2 small crabs, boiled
2 tbsps oil
4 spring onions
1 small green pepper, finely chopped
1 stick celery, finely chopped
1 clove garlic, crushed
175ml/6 fl oz mayonnaise
1 tbsp mild mustard
Dash Tabasco and Worcestershire sauce
1 piece canned pimento, drained and finely chopped
2 tbsps chopped parsley
Salt and pepper
Lettuce

---

1. To shell the crabs, first remove all the legs and the large claws by twisting and pulling them away from the body. Turn the shell over and, using your thumbs, push the body away from the flat shell. Set the body aside.

2. Remove the stomach sack and the lungs or dead man's fingers and discard them. Using a small teaspoon, scrape the brown body meat out of the flat shell.

3. Using a sharp knife, cut the body of the crab in four pieces and using a skewer, push out all the meat.

4. Crack the large claws and remove the meat. Crack the legs and remove the meat as well, leaving the small, thin legs in the shell. Set all the meat aside. Scrub the shells if wished to use for serving.

5. Heat the oil in a small frying pan. Chop the white parts of the spring onions and add to the oil with the green pepper, celery and garlic. Sauté over a gentle heat for about 10 minutes, stirring often, to soften the vegetables but not brown them. Remove from the heat and set aside. When cool, add the mayonnaise, mustard, Tabasco, Worcestershire sauce, pimento and finely chopped tops of the spring onions.

6. Spoon the reserved brown meat from the crabs back into each shell or serving dish. Mix the remaining crab meat with the dressing. Do not overmix the sauce as the crab meat should stay in large pieces. Spoon into the shells on top of the brown meat, sprinkle with chopped parsley and place the crab shells on serving plates, surrounding them with lettuce leaves. Sprinkle with parsley and serve immediately.

Spanish Potato Omelette

SERVES 2

This makes a good lunch or supper dish if served with salad and bread.

PREPARATION: 20 mins
COOKING: 30 mins

90ml/6 tbsps olive oil
225g/8oz potatoes, peeled and thinly sliced
Salt and pepper
1 medium onion, thinly sliced
4 large eggs
1 tomato, skinned, seeded and sliced
1 spring onion, chopped

---

1. Heat the oil in a large non-stick frying pan and add the potatoes. Sprinkle lightly with salt and pepper and cook over medium heat until golden brown and crisp.

2. Add the onion once the potatoes begin to brown slightly. Turn the potatoes and onions over occasionally so that they brown evenly. They should take about 20 minutes to soften and brown.

3. Beat the eggs with a pinch of salt and pepper and pour the mixture over the vegetables in the pan. Allow the mixture to run underneath the vegetables. Cook over a gentle heat until the bottom browns lightly.

Step 3 Push the eggs and potatoes back from the sides of the pan using a fork.

Step 4 Slide pan under a preheated grill to brown the top of the omelette.

4. Slide the pan under a preheated grill to brown the top of the omelette and set the eggs. Garnish with the tomato and spring onion and serve in wedges.

Buttered Prawns

SERVES 2
This makes an elegant main course, yet it's surprisingly easy.

PREPARATION: 35 mins
COOKING: 20 mins

900g/2lbs cooked unpeeled prawns
60g/2oz butter, softened
Pinch salt, white pepper and cayenne
1 clove garlic, crushed
90g/6 tbsps fine dry breadcrumbs
2 tbsps chopped parsley
60ml/4 tbsps sherry
Lemon wedges or slices, to garnish

---

1. To prepare the prawns, remove the heads and legs first.

Step 1 Remove the heads and legs from the prawns first. Remove any roe at this time.

Step 2 Pull off the tail shell and carefully remove the very end.

2. Peel off the shells, carefully removing the tail shells.

3. Remove the balck vein running down the length of the rounded side with a cocktail stick.

4. Arrange the prawns in a shallow casserole or individual dishes.

5. Combine the remaining ingredients, except the lemon garnish, mixing well.

6. Spread the mixture to completely cover the prawns and place in an oven preheated to 190°C/375°F/Gas Mark 5 for about 20 minutes, or until the butter melts and the crumbs become crisp. Garnish with lemon wedges or slices.

Sweet-Sour Fish

SERVES 2

In China this dish is almost always prepared with freshwater fish,
but sea bass is also an excellent choice.

PREPARATION: 25 mins
COOKING: 15-20 mins

---

1 sea bass, grey mullet or carp, weighing about
    900g/2lbs cleaned
1 tbsp dry sherry
Few slices fresh ginger
120g/4oz sugar
90ml/6 tbsps cider vinegar
1 tbsp soy sauce
2 tbsps cornflour
1 clove garlic, crushed
2 spring onions, shredded
1 small carrot, peeled and finely shredded
30g/1oz bamboo shoots, shredded

---

1. Rinse the fish well inside and out. Make
three diagonal cuts on each side of the fish with
a sharp knife.

2. Trim off the fins, apart from the dorsal fin on
top. Trim the tail to two neat points.

3. Bring enough water to cover the fish to the
boil in a wok. Gently lower the fish into the
boiling water and add the sherry and ginger.
Cover the wok tightly and remove at once from

Step 2 Using
kitchen
scissors, trim
off all the fins,
except for the
dorsal fin on
top.

the heat. Allow to stand 15-20 minutes to let the
fish cook in the residual heat.

4. To test if the fish is cooked, pull the dorsal
fin – if it comes off easily the fish is done. If not,
return the wok to the heat and bring to the boil.
Remove from the heat and leave the fish to
stand a further 5 minutes. Transfer the fish to a
heated serving dish and keep it warm. Take all
but 60ml/4 tbsps of the fish cooking liquid
from the wok. Add the remaining ingredients
including the vegetables and cook, stirring
constantly, until the sauce thickens. Spoon
some of the sauce over the fish to serve and
serve the rest separately.

Tomato Beef Stir-Fry

SERVES 2

East meets West in a dish that is lightning-fast to cook and tastes like a barbecue sauced stir-fry.

PREPARATION: 25 mins, plus 4 hours marinating
COOKING: 20 mins

225g/8oz sirloin or rump steak
1 clove garlic, crushed
3 tbsps wine vinegar
3 tbsps oil
Pinch sugar, salt and pepper
2 tsps ground cumin
½ small red pepper, sliced
½ small green pepper, sliced
60g/2oz baby sweetcorn
2 spring onions, shredded
Oil for frying

Tomato Sauce
2 tbsps oil
½ medium onion, finely chopped
½-1 green chilli, finely chopped
1 clove garlic, crushed
4 fresh ripe tomatoes, skinned, seeded and
   chopped
3 sprigs fresh coriander
2 tbsps tomato purée
1 bay leaf

---

1. Slice the meat thinly across the grain.

Step 1 Slice the meat thinly across the grain.

Combine in a plastic bag with the next 7 ingredients. Tie the bag and toss the ingredients inside to coat. Place in a bowl and leave for about 4 hours.

2. Heat the oil for the sauce and cook the onion, chilli and garlic to soften but not brown. Add the remaining sauce ingredients and cook for about 15 minutes over a gentle heat. Purée in a food processor until smooth.

3. Heat a large frying pan and add the meat discarding the marinade. Cook to brown and set aside. Add about 1 tbsp of oil and cook the peppers for about 2 minutes. Add the corn and onions and return the meat to the pan. Cook for a further 1 minute and add the sauce. Cook to heat through and serve immediately.

Veal with Peaches and Pine Nuts

SERVES 2

This dish is quite expensive, but very easy and quick to prepare and cook. Pork fillet or chicken breast will work equally well with this sauce.

PREPARATION: 15 mins
COOKING: 20 mins

---

2 small ripe peaches
3 tbsps brandy or sherry
4 small, thin veal escalopes
Salt and pepper
2 tbsps oil
140ml/¼ pint dry white wine
Pinch cinnamon
1 small bay leaf
2 tsps cornflour mixed with 1 tbsp water
Pinch sugar, optional
2 tbsps pine nuts, toasted

---

1. Skin the peaches by dropping them into

Step 1 Place peaches in boiling water for 30 seconds

boiling water for about 30 seconds. Remove immediately to a bowl of cold water and leave to cool completely. Use a small, sharp knife to remove the skins.

2. Cut the peaches in half, remove the stones and place the peaches in a deep bowl with the brandy or sherry. Stir the peach halves to coat them completely.

3. Heat the oil in a frying pan and fry the escalopes on both sides until golden brown. Pour on the wine and add the cinnamon, bay leaf, salt, pepper and cover the pan. Cook over a low heat for 10-15 minutes or until the veal is tender and cooked through.

4. When the veal is cooked, remove it to a serving dish and keep it warm. Add the cornflour mixture to the pan and bring to the boil. Cook until thickened and cleared.

5. Remove the peaches from the brandy and slice them. Add the peaches and the brandy to the thickened sauce mixture and bring to the boil. Allow to cook rapidly for about 1 minute. Add the sugar, if using. Spoon the peaches and sauce over the veal escalopes and sprinkle on the toasted pine nuts. Serve immediately.

Gingernut Pork Chops

SERVES 2

Ginger-flavoured biscuits give a spicy lift to pork chop gravy, thickening it at the same time.

PREPARATION: 20 mins
COOKING: 50 mins

---

2 even-sized pork chops, loin or shoulder
½ tsp ground black pepper
Pinch salt
½ tsp ground ginger
Good pinch each rubbed sage, ground
    coriander and paprika
2 tbsps oil
½ small onion, finely chopped
½ stick celery, finely chopped
1 clove garlic, crushed
200ml/7 fl oz chicken stock
6-7 gingernut biscuits, crushed

---

1. Trim the chops of any excess fat. Mix together the seasoning, herbs and spices and press the mixture firmly onto both sides of the chops.

2. Heat half the oil in a large frying pan and, when hot, add the chops. Brown on both sides and remove to a plate.

3. Heat the remaining oil in the pan and add the onion, celery and garlic. Cook to soften and pour on the stock.

4. Return the chops to the pan, cover and cook for about 30-40 minutes, or until tender.

5. When the chops are cooked, remove them to a serving dish and keep them warm. Stir the crushed gingernuts into the pan liquid and bring to the boil.

6. Stir constantly to allow the gingernuts to soften and thicken the liquid. Boil rapidly for about 3 minutes to reduce, and pour over the chops to serve.

Step 5 Use the crushed gingernuts to thicken the pan liquid. Cook slowly until dissolved.

Spiced Lamb

SERVES 2

Tender sautéed lamb is delicious in a sauce that's fragrant with herbs and spices.

PREPARATION: 25 mins, plus 4 hours marinating
COOKING: 25 mins

340g/12oz lamb neck fillet
½ tsp fresh dill, chopped
½ tsp rosemary, crushed
½ tsp fresh thyme, chopped
1 tsp mustard seeds, slightly crushed
1 bay leaf
½ tsp coarsely ground black pepper
¼ tsp ground allspice
Juice 1 lemon
140ml/¼ pint red wine
1 tbsp oil
½ small red pepper, sliced
60g/2oz button mushrooms, left whole
15g/½oz butter
1½ tbsps flour
90ml/3 fl oz beef stock
Salt

---

1. Place the lamb in a shallow dish and sprinkle on the dill, rosemary, thyme and mustard seeds. Add the bay leaf, pepper, allspice, lemon juice and wine, and stir to coat the meat thoroughly with the marinade. Leave for 4 hours in the refrigerator.

2. Heat the oil in a frying pan and add the red pepper and mushrooms and cook to soften slightly. Remove with a draining spoon.

3. Reheat the oil in the pan and add the lamb fillet, well drained and patted dry. Reserve the marinade. Brown the meat quickly on all sides to seal. Remove from the pan and set aside with the vegetables.

4. Melt the butter in the pan and when foaming add the flour. Lower the heat and cook the flour slowly until brown. Pour in the beef stock and the marinade. Bring to the boil and return the vegetables and lamb to the pan. Cook about 10-12 minutes, or until the lamb is tender, but still pink inside.

5. Slice the lamb fillet thinly on the diagonal and arrange on plates. Remove the bay leaf from the sauce and spoon over the meat.

Step 5 To serve, slice the lamb on the diagonal using a large sharp carving knife.

Roast Pigeons with Juniper Sauce

SERVES 2

This sauce will work equally well with pheasants, or venison steaks.

PREPARATION: 30 mins
COOKING: 45 mins

---

2 pigeons, dressed
120g/4oz chicken liver pâté
1 tbsp brandy
6 rashers streaky bacon
60g/2oz smoked bacon, chopped
1 onion, finely chopped
½ carrot, finely chopped
1 stick celery, finely chopped
1 tbsp juniper berries
2 tbsps flour
280ml/½ pint stock
140ml/¼ pint white wine
1 tsp tomato purée (optional)
Salt and pepper

Step 1 Remove pin feathers with tweezers or singe the pigeons over an open flame.

1. Pluck any pin feathers from the pigeons with tweezers or singe them over a gas flame.

2. Mix the pâté and brandy together and spread on the insides of each pigeon.

3. Tie the bacon on the pigeons to cover the breasts and roast them in an oven preheated to 200°C/400°F/Gas Mark 6, for 35-40 minutes.

4. Meanwhile, place the chopped bacon in a heavy-based saucepan over low heat. Cook slowly to render the fat.

5. Add the vegetables and juniper berries and cook until the vegetables begin to brown lightly.

6. Add the flour and cook until golden brown.

7. Pour the stock on gradually, stirring continuously. Bring to the boil then simmer, partially covered, for 20-25 minutes. Add more stock or water as necessary.

8. Skim the fat from the roasting pan and discard it. Add pan juices to the sauce and pour in the juices from the cavity of each pigeon.

9. Strain the sauce into a clean pan and add the wine and tomato purée, if using.

10. Bring to the boil for about 3 minutes to reduce slightly. Season with salt and pepper and serve with the pigeons.

Filled Beef Rolls

SERVES 2

This recipe is a Polish version of beef olives.

PREPARATION: 20 mins
COOKING: 45 mins

---

4 thin frying steaks, trimmed
Mustard
1 dill cucumber, cut into thin strips
60g/2oz cooked gammon steak, cut into thin
  strips
1 spring onion, shredded
2 tbsps oil
1 tbsp flour
140ml/¼ pint beef stock
2 tbsps white wine
2 tsps tomato purée
Salt and pepper
2 tbsps soured cream or thick yogurt
Chopped parsley

---

1. Place each steak between two sheets of
damp greaseproof paper and bat out with a
meat mallet or rolling pin to flatten.

2. Spread the meat thinly with some mustard
and divide the dill cucumber, gammon and
onion among all the slices.

3. Fold in about 1.25cm/½ inch of the meat
down each side. Roll the meat around the
filling and secure with cocktail sticks or tie with
fine string.

Step 3 Roll the ends of the meat over the filling to cover completely and secure with string or cocktail sticks.

4. Heat the oil in a large frying pan and when
hot, brown the beef rolls. Remove the meat and
set aside.

5. Add the flour to the pan and allow to cook
until light brown. Gradually stir in the stock
and add the wine, tomato purée, and salt and
pepper. Bring to the boil then simmer for 1
minute.

6. Return the beef rolls to the pan and spoon
over some of the sauce. Cover and cook over a
low heat for 25-30 minutes. Add more liquid as
necessary during cooking.

7. When the beef rolls are cooked, transfer
them to a serving dish and remove the cocktail
sticks or string. Spoon over the sauce and top
with the soured cream and chopped parsley.

Fillet de Porc aux Pruneaux

SERVES 2

This rich dish with its creamy sauce and wine-soaked prunes originates from the Loire region of France.

PREPARATION: 25 mins plus soaking time
COOKING: 15 mins

175g/6oz pitted no-soak prunes
225ml/8 fl oz white wine
1 small pork fillet
Seasoned flour to coat
30g/1oz butter or margarine
1½ tsps redcurrant jelly
120ml/4 fl oz double cream
Chopped parsley to garnish

---

1. Marinate the prunes in the white wine for 20 minutes.

2. Slice the pork fillet on the diagonal into 2.5 cm/1-inch thick pieces. Flatten them slightly with the palm of the hand and dredge them with seasoned flour. Melt the butter in a heavy-based pan, when it is foaming, put in the pork and cook until lightly browned on both sides.

3. Add half the soaking liquid from the prunes, cover the pan and cook very gently over a moderate heat for about 15 minutes, adding more of the wine if necessary.

4. When the pork is tender, pour the liquid into a small saucepan and bring to the boil. Reduce by about a quarter and add the redcurrant jelly. Stir until dissolved and then add the cream. Bring the sauce back to the boil and boil rapidly until the sauce is reduced and thickened slightly, pour over the meat, add the prunes and reheat. Transfer to a serving dish and sprinkle with a little chopped parsley.

Step 2 Slice the pork fillet and flatten the slices with the palm of the hand.

Step 4 Whisk the redcurrant jelly into the boiling sauce.

Garnished Pepper Steaks

SERVES 2

Serve with rice, pasta or new potatoes.

PREPARATION: 20 mins
COOKING: 15-20 mins

---

2 sirloin or rump steaks about 120g/4oz each in
    weight
1 clove garlic, crushed
Salt and freshly ground black pepper
Oil

Sauce
1 shallot, finely chopped
2 tbsps small capers
60g/2oz sliced mushrooms
1 tbsp flour
140ml/¼ pint beef stock
2 tsps German mustard
1 tsp Worcestershire sauce
60ml/4 tbsps white wine
1 tsp lemon juice
Pinch each of thyme and rosemary

Garnish
4 baby ears of corn, cut in half
½ each small green and red pepper, thinly
    sliced
2 peperonata, stem and seeds removed and cut
    in half
2 ripe tomatoes, skinned, seeded and cut into
    thin strips

Step 1 Press the steaks firmly against the base of the pan using a fish slice or spatula.

1. Rub the crushed garlic, salt and pepper into both sides of each steak. Heat a large frying pan and brush the surface lightly with oil. Place the steaks in the hot pan and press them down firmly with a fish slice to seal. Turn over and repeat. Remove the steaks to a plate and add 1 tbsp of oil to the pan.

2. Add the shallot, capers, and mushrooms and cook for about 1 minute. Sprinkle on the flour and cook to brown slightly. Pour on the stock and stir well. Add the remaining sauce ingredients and bring to the boil.

3. Add the corn and peppers to the sauce and return the steaks to the pan. Cook for 6-8 minutes or until the steaks are cooked to taste. Add the remaining ingredients to the sauce. Transfer the steaks to a heated serving plate, and spoon the sauce over the steaks.

Duck in Caper Sauce

SERVES 2

*A sweet-sour sauce with the tang of capers is a perfect accompaniment
to a rich meat such as duck.*

PREPARATION: 20 mins, plus 1-2 hours standing
COOKING: 1½ hours

---

1 × 1.8kg/4lb duck
1 clove garlic, crushed
Salt and pepper
1 tbsp oil
45g/1½oz butter or margarine
280ml/½ pint chicken stock
140ml/¼ pint water
60g/4 tbsps sugar
1 tbsp vinegar or lemon juice
4 tsps cornflour mixed with 2 tbsps water
90ml/6 tbsps capers

---

1. Rub the cavity of the duck with the crushed garlic and sprinkle in salt and pepper. Leave to stand in a cool place 1-2 hours but do not refrigerate.

2. Heat the oil in a heavy frying pan or roasting tin and when hot add the butter or margarine. Prick the duck skin all over with a sharp fork then brown on all sides in the hot fat. Transfer the duck to a saucepan or flameproof casserole.

3. Pour over the stock, cover and simmer over a medium heat for about 1½ hours, or until the duck is tender.

4. Meanwhile, heat the water and sugar together slowly in a small, heavy-based saucepan until the sugar dissolves.

5. Once the sugar is dissolved, turn up the heat and boil rapidly until it caramelizes. Remove from the heat and carefully pour in the vinegar or lemon juice. It will splutter violently. Add several spoonfuls of the cooking liquid from the duck and set the caramel over a medium heat. Allow the mixture to come to the boil, stirring constantly.

6. When the duck is tender, remove it to a heated serving dish. Skim off the fat from the cooking liquid and discard. Add several spoonfuls of the duck cooking liquid to the cornflour mixture. Return to the rest of the liquid and bring to the boil. Add the capers and stir over a high heat until the sauce clears and thickens. Add the caramel and stir until the sauce is thick.

7. Cut the duck into portions or serve whole and spoon over some of the sauce. Serve the rest of the sauce separately.

Brown Bread Crumble

The unusual crumble topping on this dessert is simple to make, high in fibre and very tasty.
Serve with custard or cream for a treat.

PREPARATION: 15 mins
COOKING: 20 mins

175g/6oz cooking apples, cored and sliced
120g/4oz raspberries
60g/2oz fresh wholemeal breadcrumbs
60g/2oz rolled oats
45g/1½oz light muscovado sugar
½ tsp ground cinnamon
¼ tsp ground cardamom
45g/1½oz butter or margarine

---

1. Arrange the apple slices in a small pie dish and scatter the raspberries over the top.

2. Put the breadcrumbs, oats, sugar and spices in a large bowl. Mix together well to distribute the spices evenly.

3. Add the butter and rub into the mixture until well mixed.

4. Spoon the topping over the prepared fruit and smooth the top with a spoon.

5. Bake in an oven preheated to 190°C/375°F/ Gas Mark 5, for 20-25 minutes or until the topping is lightly browned and the filling piping hot.

Blackcurrant Snow with Mint

SERVES 2

This simple dessert, which is quick and easy to make, looks very effective when served in tall glasses with langue de chat biscuits.

PREPARATION: 15 mins

60g/2oz fresh or frozen blackcurrants
3 tbsps granulated sugar
1 egg white
90ml/3 fl oz whipping cream
90ml/3 fl oz natural yogurt
1 tbsp chopped fresh mint

Garnish
Whole sprigs fresh mint

1. Combine the blackcurrants and 1 tbsp of the sugar in a small, heavy-based pan. Cook slowly until juice forms and the blackcurrants soften. Set aside to cool completely.

2. When the blackcurrants are cool, whisk the egg white until stiff but not dry.

3. Gradually whisk in the remaining sugar. Whisk well in between each addition of sugar until stiff peaks form and the egg white is smooth and glossy.

4. Whip the cream until thick, and combine with the yogurt.

5. Fold the egg white into the cream and yogurt mixture along with the cooled blackcurrants and the chopped mint. Do not over-fold, the mixture should look marbled.

6. Spoon into individual serving dishes and garnish with the whole sprigs of mint. Make and eat the same day.

Cherry Compôte

SERVES 2

This makes a special, elegant pudding, but an easy one, too. The contrast of hot brandied cherries and cold ice cream or whipped cream is sensational.

PREPARATION: 10 mins
COOKING: 10 mins

340g/12oz canned black, pitted cherries, juice
    reserved
1-2 tbsps sugar
2 tbsps brandy
Vanilla ice cream or whipped cream, to serve

---

1. Combine the cherry juice with the sugar and heat through to dissolve it. Add the cherries to the juice.

2. Pour the brandy into a separate saucepan. Heat the brandy and ignite with a match. Combine the brandy with the fruit and leave

Step 2 Add the flaming brandy to the cherries and leave until the flames die down naturally.

until the flames die down naturally.

3. Serve the fruit over ice cream or spoon into serving dishes and top with whipped cream. Serve immediately.

Index